Ten Poems from Norfolk

Candlestick Press

Published by:
Candlestick Press,
Diversity House, 72 Nottingham Road, Arnold, Nottingham NG5 6LF, UK
www.candlestickpress.co.uk

Design and typesetting by Craig Twigg

Printed by Bayliss Printing Company Ltd of Worksop, UK

Selection and Introduction © Helen Ivory and Martin Figura, 2025

Cover illustration © Louise Stebbing, 2025
https://www.louisestebbingprintmaker.com/

Candlestick Press monogram © Barbara Shaw, 2008

© Candlestick Press, 2025

ISBN 978 1 913627 64 5

Acknowledgements

The poems in this pamphlet are reprinted from the following books, all by permission of the publishers listed unless stated otherwise. Every effort has been made to trace the copyright holders of the poems published in this book. The editor and publisher apologise if any material has been included without permission, or without the appropriate acknowledgement, and would be glad to be told of anyone who has not been consulted.

Thanks are due to all the copyright holders cited below for their kind permission.

Moniza Alvi, *At the Time of the Partition* (Bloodaxe Books, 2013) www.bloodaxebooks.com. Martin Figura, poem first published in this anthology by kind permission of the author. Jen Hadfield, *Places of Poetry* (Oneworld Publications, 2020) by kind permission of the author. Matt Howard, *Broadlands* (Bloodaxe Books, 2024), www.bloodaxebooks.com. Helen Ivory, poem first published in this anthology by kind permission of the author. John Kett, *Tha's a Rum'un Bor! Norfolk Verse* (Baron Publishing, 1973) by kind permission of the Estate of John Kett. Andrew McDonnell, *55 Devotionals (Against Erasure)* (Broken Sleep Books, 2025) by kind permission of the author. Esther Morgan, *Translating John Crome: Through Sight to Insight*, ed. Andrew Moore & Clive Scott, (UEA Publishing Project, 2025) by kind permission of the author. George Szirtes, *New & Collected Poems* (Bloodaxe Books, 2008) www.bloodaxebooks.com.

All permissions cleared courtesy of Dr Suzanne Fairless-Aitken
c/o Swift Permissions swiftpermissions@gmail.com.

Where poets are no longer living, their dates are given.

Introduction

Of course, ten poems are not enough to say something about a county – but hear these voices speak to you from this shifting landscape. A place of water, inland dunes, marsh mist and skies that stretch right to the edge of the page.

Before the last Ice Age, Norfolk was joined to the Continent and mammoth bones have been latterly found on our coastline. Time was, it took a day to sail the 113 miles to the Netherlands, and because of impassable land, four days to travel the 117 miles to London. Dutch engineers came here to help manage the waterlogged land, and refugees or 'Strangers' from the Spanish Netherlands fled here in the 16th century, bringing with them skills in textile weaving which reanimated the county after the Black Death.

Fragments of this history of land movement and people movement float through into many of these poems. Environmentalist Matt Howard writes of the management of dykes in land "below sea level" – 'dyke' deriving from the Old Dutch name for 'dam'. There is a keen sense of Norfolk as a home that must be journeyed towards – Moniza Alvi brings her mother's story of migration with her into the "Norfolk light" and Camilla Doyle returns to a place whose very shadows "Are more myself than I myself can be".

It is important to include the richness of the Norfolk dialect and local words which are rare finds these days, save for in books like *How to Speak Fen*, which Jen Hadfield celebrates. This poem talks of "hand-me-down weather", and now parts of the coast are falling away due to rising sea levels, land and water are on the move again. We wanted to include headmaster poet John Kett's poem 'Ole Shuck' which is written in pure Broad Norfolk, so slow you down and read it out loud. Shuck is the ghostly dog of English folklore who has long been sighted round here even by teetotallers, it must be said! But that's a wholly different story.

Helen Ivory and Martin Figura

The Water Map

It's all water here, or not water
subject to engineering and weather.
You open out an old map on the grass
clock the straight cut of drains
and all those little windpumps
pushing up like flowers.

The rivers of flat country are silent.
Draw in close and feel the Yare move
twelve centimetres a second
as water eases from the land
into an aquifer of chalk.
Imagine this deep in the fabric of the map.

Now spread your wings
hover as a sickle-taloned kestrel
above the sunken trees of Doggerland
then plummet sharp into the marram-knitted dunes
caught in ink by the cartographer
before sea was risen all beyond itself to claim them.

Helen Ivory

Winter Wings

(Wymondham Abbey)

How brilliantly the sun
for a moment strides
through the glass
then hides
in deep
recesses
in the very aisles
it so briefly caresses,

so the heart stops and restarts
without noticing
it has stopped:
a swing
lurching,
an eye lost
in mid-blink, dark birds
in full-flight, swimming through dust.

George Szirtes

Study of Flints

"Study of flint stones from Nature by Crome Painted as a lesson for the Misses Jerningham of Cossey Hall nr. Norwich"

There is always something –
even if it's only this:
its chalk-white surface, a black cracked-open heart.

The kind you might kick
a few yards down a track
but picked up, looked at,

no, *really* looked at
until this little canvas
hums with its presence.

Just so, says our Master-of-the-Stones,
not everything worthy of notice
has to be beautiful

fixing us with a gaze
neutral and constant
as the light in a north-facing room.

Feel the truth of that sink in –
beneath the lace and watered silk
of our positions

beneath the calico and skin
beneath the flesh, beneath even, the bone:
how sacred we are and nothing special.

Esther Morgan

See how the rotary ditcher is

making all this, with each pass
the sun jagging off steel, its cutting angles
led by a cyclops laser eye, profiling –

our hauled bulk and radials
gnarling a dream of mud, freshwater,
spuming spoil, excavating great lengths

of foot drains, shallow pools, fresh lymph nodes
off the main dykes. There's a new fringe
already waking in the wing mirrors,

micro topographies of soil, cleft and lifted
marsh falling back as more of itself. This
nowhere-middle of Berney, below sea level,

the fag-end of a heathen summer,
thundering under a slab of Broadland sky.
These muck scars will not last.

Each pass is to pass on. What is and will yet be.
Here's grazing for wigeon and pink-feet
in a matter of weeks, where just a season will yield

tussocks of redshank, lapwing scrapes,
chicks about the midge larvae in new wet edges.
We're no more than tending a body of water

that'll bloom the tumbling displays to come,
spread primaries mirroring in pools,
flashing the sky's own outstretched offerings.

There's all the earth moved. The key turned,
now the heavy-legged comedown from the cab,
back to the hardstanding under your boots.

Matt Howard

Cloth

Think of this city as cloth, its people as remnants,
its flinty churches built from merchant wool.

Throwsterers, twisterers and wool-combers
came here from the low countries with their canaries
and this city remade itself in finery.

Who amongst us has never been a stranger
at some shore, like a hopeful little boat.
How does anyone end up anywhere?

When I was a boy, elsewhere, motherless
and all but gone to the storm, I was given
as a small act of kindness, a yellow shirt

a canary at its breast. It became
my second skin, the canary singing
brightly to my heart and when

years later as a man, I found myself
lonely and lost again, the canary
remembered and sang and the song

gathered me in - one tiny loose thread.
Home isn't always where you started from.

Martin Figura

Ole Shuck

Yew wanter know about Ole Shuck?
Well, bor, I reckon yew're in luck;
   Tha's good yew hap't on me.
Corse if yew arsk'd some I c'ld naame
Old Nick'ld hang his hid in shaame –
   They tell sich lies, y'see!

Now, 'bout Ole Shuck . . . Yew know that laane
What run beside the ole marsh drain
   Jus' pas' the pub up there?
I tell yew, tha's where he hang out,
When there in't no-one else about
   Yew'll see'im, I declare.

Some say he ony come the night
The mune is full, an' shinin' bright –
   But tha's all squit, I say.
When tha's pitch dark yew wanter go,
When neither mune yit stars don't show
   Yew'll see him on his way.

One night, b' that ole pollard tree,
Thet gret dawg he come arter me.
   I'll lay I nigh on shruck!
An' then he went a-pantin' paast;
I felt his breath, an icy blaast –
   Ah, bor, I'a met Ole Shuck!

An' many a time (I tell no lie)
In that there laane he'a passed me by,
   His red jaws all a-foam.
. . . Tha's straange I never see him, though,
When up there t'the pub I go –
   Tha's when I'm comin' hoom!

John Kett (1917 – 2010)

The Return

(Cathedral Close, Norwich)

Long wandering years, you're past! – I'm home again.
   These winding alleys and these high flint walls
   On which the little creeping-toadflax sprawls
Have had the power to draw me back, to strain
Me close and safe – kinder than human arms.
   These bells whose leisured chimes ring in the hour,
   Not having changed like human tones, had power
To call from far through griefs and through alarms.

Oh, people change! I'm changed myself; but these,
These lanes for loitering in, these apple-trees,
   Gardens for reading in – yes, all I see,
The wheeling rooks, the tall stone gates that throw
Strong shadows on the quiet paths below,
   Are more myself than I myself can be.

Camilla Doyle (1888 – 1944)

The Weighing

She tells me how, when I wasn't feeding well
she'd take me down the lane to her neighbour
the other English woman, an inspector of schools.
My mother would stand on this lady's scales
with – and then without me.
So that was how I was weighed

at that difficult time in Pakistan.
1954. The sky was burning blue.
It was later, a few years later, that I started
as they say, to thrive.
Am I thriving now? I ask myself.
What do I weigh in my flesh and bones –

in the secret inside the scales?
The difference then between my mother
with and without me – was it infinitesimal?
Now she glances at me as if in wonderment
as I sit in the armchair opposite
and Norfolk light floods the care home windows.

By a sleight of hand her story
becomes my own.
I pass it on here – a little of it.

Moniza Alvi

Evensong

> *'When the river's full, don't trust anyone'*
> WH Barrett's grandfather in *How to Speak Fen* by Michael Rouse (2018)

> *'Lighten our darkness, we beseech thee, O Lord*
> *and defend us from all perils and dangers of this night'*
> *The Third Collect*, Book of Common Prayer (1662)

> *'The number of insects is falling at such a perilous rate that if*
> *nothing is done to halt the decline, our own future could be at risk'*
> Natural History Museum (2019)

Child, whatever
weather is our hellish hand-me-down to you,
if you can forgive us, it'll be a miracle.
But when I imagine the tide coming in: the way it
comes in and comes in, and stays
in like a bolt shot home, fen
filling up like a
waterbed, I pray,
literally
pray, here at Evensong, this:
that at least the last of the fenfolk might
creep back at nightfall through the shining
fields, volty with damselflies: barbubblers and
buttleebumps, pale grey Tiddy-mun,
Hod-me-dod, the pilgrim snail –
the patched bundle of his shell wagging on
his patient back – and gentle giant
Tom Hickathrift –
all led by Lantern-Man
like refugees
across an abandoned border –
Owd Sally to what's left of the high ground,
Jack to the flood. And until the spalt vanes of the
windpump snap like celery in a shuft
of wind, may it bail
eel-thick water in stelches,
and when storms turn fen-blows
to brown paint, make for the

Isle, for that cobweb spun
of soft white stone where anyone
may light
a candle; with
whatever rope ladder you can spin
from what you could salvage –
eelskin and psalm
caul and song –

Jen Hadfield

Barbubblers – featherless birds / *Buttleebumps* – bitterns / *Tiddy-mun* – a little grey man dressed in white. Fen people would ask for his help when the cottages flooded. His answer was like the call of a peewit / *Hod-me-dod* – snail-like creature / *Lantern Man* – like the Will-o'-the wisp, Lantern Man would lead the unwary to their doom / *Owd Sally* – a hare / *Jack* – a small pike / *spalt* – brittle, easy to snap / *shuft* – a sudden gust of wind / *stelches* – to talk in short phrases with long pauses between / *fen-blows* – dust storms.

from *How to Speak Fen: Lore and Language of the Fens* by Michael Rouse (Ely History Publications, 2018).

Devotional for the Acle Straight

Farmland passes on the horizon, the soft steam of a sugar beet factory hangs above the flatland and seems to move at the pace of the coach. Orange curtains hang against the snow, the purple of the fields and the frozen puddles of water that I can imagine my dead dad's ghost breaking with his walking stick.

Worldly things seem so brittle, so precarious: the television masts, the fleet of white hire vans surrounded by floodlights, the two-carriage train high on the bank. We pass single drivers going the other way, the coach driver catching one last look at them in his side mirrors.

Behind us, Great Yarmouth is lighting its lights against the coming tides.

Andrew McDonnell